EXCITING PROVEN STRATEGIES TO MAKE YOUR BAG A *BRAND*

Bag it Right

EXCITING PROVEN STRATEGIES
TO MAKE YOUR BAG A *BRAND*

Bag it Right

PUNIT SINGHAL

INDIA'S #1 IMPACT BAG BRANDING EXPERT

Worldwide Published by
Pendown Press

PENDOWN PRESS

An ISO 9001 & ISO 14001 Certified Co.,

Regd. Office: 2525/193, 1st Floor, Onkar Nagar-A,

Tri Nagar, Delhi-110035

Ph.: 09350849407, 09312235086

E-mail: info@pendownpress.com

Branch Office: 1A/2A, 20, Hari Sadan, Ansari Road,

Daryaganj, New Delhi-110002

Ph.: 011-45794768

Website: PendownPress.com

First Edition: 2023

ISBN: 978-93-5554-618-0

Layout and Cover Designed by Pendown Graphics Team

Printed and Bound in India by Thomson Press India Ltd.

Gratitude

This book is dedicated to almighty Krishna.

My wife Anita, my daughter Kanak, has been a constant source of love and support, always by my side and giving me the time I need to write.

My brother Piyush and Mohit, who always inspires me to grow further.

My role model, my father Mr. P.M. Agarwal, who is founder of Jagannath Group and an Udyog Ratan awardee.

Additionally, I would like to express my gratitude to my Guru Akshar Yadav, who has bestowed upon me this amazing power to reach millions of people.

Contents

About Me

I am a Chartered Accountant by profession, and have always had a desire to be involved in business, being born into a business family. I completed my graduation from Rajasthan university.

Originally hailing from a small place in Jaipur, called Chomu.

In 2018, I joined the packaging business as a trainee, working alongside my brother Mohit. This journey of understanding packaging and solving people's problems has been consistently amazing.

I always look at things with a solution, I am a firm believer that every lock is made with a key.

Opening

Hello my name is Punit, I am a Chartered Accountant and hold a Bachelor of Commerce degree from Commerce College, Rajasthan University. I am a second-generation entrepreneur involved in the manufacturing of PP/BOPP woven sacks. The Jagannath Group, is a leader in flexible packaging, covering every aspect from start to finish can be said as every flexible solution under one roof.

After completing my CA, I had the desire to gain industry exposure, so I decided to do a job for two years. During this time, I appeared for campus placements and secured a position at E&Y with a package of 7 lakhs Per Annum.

However, It was a heartbreak, because during my previous experience working with Jagannath, I had noticed that we were paying higher salaries to our staff.

So, I decided to join the flexible packaging industry immediately.

This was a good decision overall, and soon the group entrusted me with individual responsibility for the BOPP woven sack division.

I excel in working with numbers and love playing with them.

During my learning phase, I worked at the grass-roots level, attending to machines and observing all the processes first hand. I actively engaged with suppliers and customers, addressing their queries and concerns. Additionally, I had the opportunity to be part of the new Research and Development team.

The current Indian woven sack industry faces numerous challenges, including lower volumes, high entry costs, multiple packaging options, developmental costs and timelines, value additions, and safe delivery and storage. My experience working at the grassroots level provided me with so much knowledge about my product, the industry and alternatives solutions. This knowledge enabled us to challenge these challenges and establish ourselves as the only Indian company to receive the Udyog Ratan Award and leading SME Exporter Awards in 2022.

Our packaging offers high dimensional stability at the lowest cost, highest performance and fastest time-to-market.

Currently, I am on a mission to share this comprehensive knowledge and create a world-class packaging experience in the Indian woven sack market.

Why read the book?

I have been working with many highly experienced packaging professionals with diverse backgrounds and have witnessed their deep understanding and ability to identify the right packaging solutions.

Many companies hire packaging professions to ensure they receive packaging that meets their requirements without exceeding or falling short of specifications.

Many packaging courses are creating an army of professionals who assist companies in choosing the right packaging solutions.

However, not all companies have access to these professionals. Some companies may not have a dedicated packaging department and view packaging as a one-time project.

This situation creates a gray area because if you lack access to technical knowledge, you may rely on the expertise of your vendor or simply follow what your competitors are doing.

But is approach always the right one?

Does your vendor guide you with effective packaging or provide sub-standard packaging?

Based on my close collaboration with several Indian companies, I observed that this often leads to sub-standard packaging or packaging that is or either expensive or exceeds the required specifications. As a packaging company with 26 years of experience in flexible packaging, I must candidly state that the performance of Indian packaging is not up to par.

Packaging is the most important aspect of 360-degree branding space. It plays a vital role in creating brand loyalty and serves as the initial point of contact during actual sales. It is my sincere desire that packaging on retail shelves in India have a more appealing appearance. that many companies are investing really good amounts of money but not getting effective packaging for their products. Nonetheless, I hope that Indian packaging companies will operate with honesty and integrity, delivering the appropriate packaging solutions that meet your needs. With this mini book, my aim is to guide companies in achieving the right packaging by sharing secrets which they should know.. Let this book be your packaging guide, to get the most suitable, best-quality and reasonably-priced packaging solutions.

During one of my meetings with a multinational corporation (MNC), after finalizing an order and having a productive discussion, I had the opportunity to have a coffee with the Group MD.

He asked me one question that left a deep impact on me:-

He asked, "Punit, why should we buy from you?"

In response, I simply listed the following reasons:

Our company has a 26-year history.

We offer the best quality of bags

We have provided the most competitive rates among the five bids you received.

Although, the meeting went well, but I couldn't shake off the question spinning in my head.

Was that the only reason why someone should choose to work with me? I was not satisfied with my answer.

From that point onward, the trajectory of our business and our lives shifted as we embarked on a quest to find the answer to that question. And now, I firmly believe that we have a bunch of reasons why one should choose to work with us.

It was a simple question that transformed our perspective and influenced our actions.

Foreword

"Bag it Right" is an eye-opening book that sheds light on several preconceived notions that many of us have about woven sacks. I highly recommend anyone associated with the printing, packaging, and recycling industry to read this book and gain valuable information and knowledge from Punit Singhal, an undisputed thought leader in the Indian packaging industry.

~Rittick Poddar,

Procurement Officer at ITC Limited.

Chapter 1

Welcome to the World of Packaging

In today's fast-paced dynamic consumer-driven market, the significance of packaging cannot be overstated in determining the success of a product. It serves as a guardian, protecting goods from the rigors of transportation and preserving their quality and freshness. But, packaging is not merely a functional necessity; it is also a powerful marketing tool that can make or break a brand. This is the point where most business fails.

Welcome to the fascinating realm of packaging, where science meets art, and functionality meets aesthetics. This guide endeavors to equip you with a comprehensive understanding of the intricate world of packaging, with a particular emphasis on woven sacks—a versatile packaging material widely used in industries, including FMCG, food, feed, chemicals and more.

Packaging is more than just a wrapper; it embodies the essence of a product, serving as its captivating face that communicates with consumers. It is the first point of contact, the visual representation of what lies within. Effective packaging captivates attention, creates desire, and compels consumers to choose one product over another. The art of packaging design, combined with the science of material selection, is a delicate balance that can make a significant difference in the market success of a product.

The printing industry occupies a vital position within the realm of packaging, as it breathes life into design concepts, transforming ideas into tangible forms that deeply resonate with consumers. From vibrant colours to intricate patterns, the printing industry bestows the final touches that make packaging visually appealing, informative, and captivatingly engaging.

Within the vast landscape of packaging materials, woven sacks emerge as remarkable contenders due to their exceptional attributes. Woven sacks, also known as polypropylene sacks or PP bags, are renowned for their notable strength, durability, and versatility. They are made from polypropylene, a material that combines the best of both worlds—strength and flexibility, woven sacks offer the ideal combination of desirable properties.

The applications of woven sacks are extensive and diverse. Whether it's carrying rice and grains or packaging chemicals and industrial goods, woven sacks have consistently demonstrated their reliability and effectiveness in various sectors. Their robustness allows for safe storage solution, efficient transportation, and protection against environmental factors such as moisture, UV rays, and pests.

Choosing the appropriate packaging material is crucial for businesses, as it impacts product quality, customer satisfaction, and brand reputation. However, navigating the packaging landscape can be overwhelming, with numerous materials, terminology, and considerations to take into account. That's why this guide is here to demystify the world of packaging and equip you with valuable insights that will empower you to make well-informed decisions.

Woven Sacks Manufacturing Process

Woven sacks are widely used in the packaging industry due to their strength and durability. In this section, we will explore the manufacturing process of woven sacks.

Weaving

Feeding flat tapes sequentially through weaving machines with warp and weft threads to produce a woven fabric.

Bag making and Packing

Cutting the woven fabric into the desired shape and size, followed by rbailing and storage.

1   2   3   4

Extrusion

Extrusion of polypropylene granules into flat tapes of various widths and thicknesses.

Lamination

The woven fabric then undergoes lamination with BOPP or LDPE films depending on type of bag required.

Chapter 2

Understanding
the Secrets of Woven Sacks

In this chapter, I will guide you through the fascinating world of woven sacks, delving into their composition, characteristics, and various types. Additionally, I will decode the essential terminology used in the packaging industry to help you gain a comprehensive understanding of woven sacks and make well-informed decisions when selecting them for your packaging needs.

The Composition and Characteristics of Woven Sacks

Woven sacks are made from polypropylene fabric, specifically PP 030SG, which is renowned for its strength and versatility. This fabric is created by weaving polypropylene tapes together in a crosshatch pattern on a circular loom, resulting in fabric in tabular or flat form.

Circular loom

Here are the key characteristics of woven sacks:

1. **Strength and Durability:** Woven sacks are renowned for their exceptional strength and durability. They are capable of withstanding heavy loads, resisting tearing and puncturing, and providing excellent protection for packaged goods. These bags are available in a capacity range from kg to metric tons (MT).

2. **Flexibility:** Despite their strength, woven sacks also offer flexibility, enabling them to conform to various shapes and sizes. This characteristic makes them suitable for packaging a wide range of products and facilitates their transportation via different modes.

3. **Moisture Resistance:** Woven sacks possess inherent moisture resistance, shielding the contents from dampness and damage caused by moisture. However,

for complete moisture protection, additional measures such as lamination or liners may be required.

Exploring Different Types of Woven Sacks

Woven sacks come in various types, each designed to meet specific packaging needs. These sacks can come in white, transparent, or of any other colour. Masterbatches are used in conjunction with polypropylene to give colour to fabric.

Let's take a closer look at some commonly used types:

1. **Standard Woven Sacks:** These are the most commonly used woven sacks and boast exceptional strength and durability. They are suitable for packaging a wide range of products, including grains, rice, flour, animal feed, and more.

2. **BOPP Laminated Woven Sacks:** Biaxially Oriented Polypropylene (BOPP) laminated woven sacks have an extra layer of BOPP film that is laminated onto the outer surface of the sack. This provides enhanced moisture resistance, improved printability for branding purposes, and a glossy or matte finish appearance.

3. **Metalized woven sacks:** These sacks combine the strength and durability of woven sacks with a metallic film layer. This metallic layer offers outstanding barrier properties against moisture, UV rays, and oxygen, making them ideal for packaging products that require extended shelf life and protection from external

elements. Furthermore, this enhances the branding and appearance of bag to a higher level. The use of gold and silver inks can further enhance the visual appeal and texture of the bag.

4. **Gusseted Woven Sacks:** Gusseted woven sacks have expandable sides or folds that allow for increased volume and capacity. They are commonly used for packaging bulky or irregularly shaped products, such as fertilizers, chemicals, and construction materials.

    These bags helps in better branding on side and make handling (loading/unloading easy).

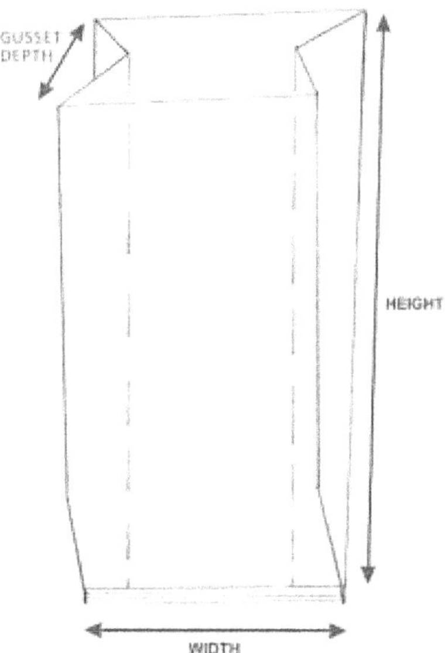

Image Showing Gusset Bag

5. **Perforated Woven Sacks:** These sacks are equipped with tiny perforations or holes, which allow for improved airflow. They are ideal for packaging products that require ventilation, such as vegetables, fruits, and other perishable items. These holes may be difficult to discern with naked eyes.

6. **Handle or D cut Bags:** These bags are come with robust handles, facilitating effortless carrying and transportation. The handles are typically made from durable materials, ensuring strength and durability. Handle or D-cut BOPP woven bags offer a convenient and practical packaging solution.

Chapter 3

Decoding Essential Terminology

To make informed decisions about woven sacks, it is essential to understand the terminology commonly used in the packaging industry. Let's decode some of the key terms:

1. **Weight Specifications:** Weight specifications pertain measurement of the weight of woven fabric per square meter used in sack production. It is often expressed in grams per square meter (GSM). A higher GSM value indicates a denser and stronger fabric.

2. **Tapes:** Woven sack is made of tapes woven together in a sequential manner. These tapes, typically composed of polypropylene, are woven together to create a robust and flexible fabric. They contribute to the strength, tear resistance, and dimensional stability to the woven sacks, ensuring their reliability for packaging various products across different industries. The weight and specifications of the tapes vary depending on the specific use case.

Mesh Pattern

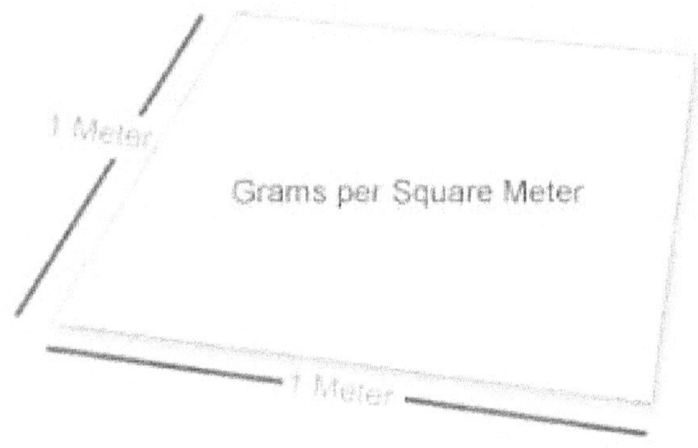

3. **Denier:** Denier is a unit of measurement that indicates the thickness or fineness of individual tapes within the woven fabric. A higher denier value indicates thicker and stronger fibers, contributing to the overall robustness of the sack.

4. **Weave:** Weave refers to the pattern formed by

interlacing polypropylene tapes in the fabric. Common weave patterns include flat or circular weaves. Each pattern possesses distinct characteristics, such as strength, flexibility, and breathability.

5. **Lamination:** Lamination entails applying an additional layer of film, typically composed of PP and LDPE,onto the woven sack's surface. This supplementary layer enhances printability, provides increased moisture resistance, and offers protection against external elements. Furthermore, BOPP or Metalized BOPP can also be laminated onto this layer for additional benefits.

6. **BOPP:** Biaxially Oriented Polypropylene (BOPP) is a versatile film commonly used in packaging. It boasts exceptional clarity, high tensile strength, and moisture resistance. BOPP film is used to laminate after printing, and as a protective layer in packaging, providing both functionality and visual appeal.

7. **Rotogravure printing:** It is a high-quality and precise printing technique extensively employed in the packaging industry. It involves engraving the desired image onto a cylinder, which then transfers the ink onto the substrate, such as BOPP film. Rotogravure printing yields vibrant colours, fine details, and consistent results. It is particularly suitable for large-volume printing and is widely used for making BOPP woven sack.

8. **Flexographic printing is a versatile and cost-effective printing method widely used to make PP Bags.** It involves flexible printing plates that transfer ink onto woven fabric surface. Flexographic printing enables quick production turnaround, excellent colour reproduction, and is well-suited for high-speed printing operations. Additionally, it is suitable for low volumes.

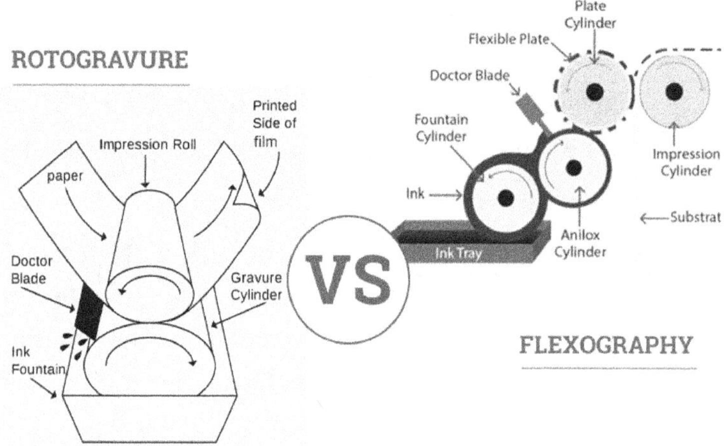

9. **Cylinders:** Cylinders are cylindrical employed used in printing, particularly in the packaging industry where they are used in rotogravure printing machines. These cylinders are engraved or coated with ink, enabling precise and consistent transfer of ink onto the substrate, resulting in high-quality prints.

10. **Tensile:** Tensile strength is a crucial characteristic of woven sacks as it signifies their ability to withstand pulling or stretching forces without breaking. It ensures the sacks can endure the stresses encountered during storage, transportation, and handling. Higher tensile strength in woven sacks indicates greater durability and reliability, providing optimal protection for packaged goods.

11. **Ash content:** Ash content refers to the residue remaining after burning a woven sack. In layman's terms, it indicates the impurities or non-combustible materials present in the sack's fabric. A lower ash content signifies a cleaner and purer material, which is desirable in woven sacks as it ensures higher quality and reduces the risk of contamination to the packaged goods.

By understanding these essential terms, you will be better equipped to assess the quality, durability, and suitability of woven sacks for your specific packaging needs.

Chapter 4

Avoiding Costly Mistakes

Introduction

In this chapter, we will delve into the common mistakes made by companies when selecting packaging materials and examine their impact on product quality and overall costs. By gaining an understanding of these pitfalls and implementing effective strategies, you can make informed decisions that enhance both quality and cost-effectiveness in your packaging choices. With our 27 years of experience, we have and successfully encountered these challenges.

Mistakes in Packaging Material Selection	Solutions
Inadequate Assessment of Product Requirements	Conduct a comprehensive assessment of product characteristics, environmental factors, and handling/transportation needs. Take into account factors such as weight, size, fragility, moisture sensitivity, temperature fluctuations, and stacking/transportation challenges. A poor assessment can result in ineffective packaging. It is necessary to evaluate whether a PP bag or BOPP bag is required, whether a natural or milky colour is preferred, and whether gusseted or non-gusseted bags are necessary. Additionally, for smaller bags, an assessment is required to determine whether handle bags or D cut bags should be used. There are numerous case studies I may tell you where wrong assessment lead to many problems.

Compromising on Packaging Material Quality	Prioritize quality over cost and establish partnerships with reputable and well-established suppliers. Implement rigorous quality control measures to ensure consistency in the packaging materials. Compromising on packaging material quality, especially when it comes to PP (Polypropylene) bags, can have detrimental consequences. Inferior quality PP bags may lack sufficient strength and durability, resulting to tearing, breakage, or compromised protection for the packaged goods. Investing in high-quality PP bags guarantees product integrity, customer satisfaction, and prevents potential losses due to product damage or spoilage. There are 11 points that are taken in consideration for a robust bag.
Overlooking Cost-Effectiveness	Balance cost and quality by exploring volume discounts, bulk purchasing, and implementing efficient packaging design to minimize waste. There are multiple approaches to achieve this. One approach is PPP framework. This framework helps you identify price volatility and gain access to real time price information. This gives you an edge over competition and you always gets lowest cost.
Inadequate Supplier Evaluation	Failing to thoroughly evaluate potential woven sack suppliers can lead to unreliable partnerships or the procurement of poor-quality products. It is crucial to assess suppliers based on various factors such as reputation, certifications, quality control processes, and adherence to ethical and social responsibility standards. It is always advisable to work with companies that prioritize long-term relations and can provide expert guidance on packaging solutions.
Disregarding Regulatory Compliance:	Neglecting to ensure compliance of the chosen bags with relevant industry regulations and standards,such as the Legal Metrology Act, Food Safety and Standard Act of India, Trademark Act, Agmark Laws, and others, can result in legal issues, penalties, and delays in product distribution. It is essential to prioritize compliance to maintain regulatory adherence and avoid costly consequences. According to a recent study, it was found that 74% bags had some irregularities due to poor awareness among bag manufacturers and brand owners. Therefore, it is imperative to stay informed about the applicable regulations and work with reputable suppliers who prioritize compliance to mitigate any potential risks or complications.

Counterfeiting and Brand Security:	One must be aware of the risks associated with counterfeiting in the woven sack industry. Working with unorganized or non-genuine woven sacks manufacturers can result in product tampering, brand infringement, and compromised product security. It is crucial to source woven sacks from trusted suppliers to ensure authenticity and safeguard brand reputation. In case of printed bags, it is crucial to have a proper mechanism in place to control printing dies and minimize wastage of printed bags. Surprisingly, more than 80% manufacturers have no control over these aspects, which significantly contributes to recurring counterfeiting problems. Additionally, working with unorganized or non-genuine manufacturers further exacerbates this issue..
Bad Artwork	In case of printed bags,the artwork for flexo or rotogravure printing plays a crucial role. Unfortunately, this aspect is often neglected during the bag manufacturing process. Many manufacturers either resort to copying other brands designs or create basic artwork that fails to engage customers effectively. Neglecting the importance of artwork can prove to be a costly mistake. We will discuss in detail on this point in upcoming chapters.

By avoiding these mistakes and implementing the suggested solutions, businesses can gain control over their packaging material selection, ensuring optimal product quality, cost-effectiveness, and sustainability. We have numerous case studies where companies have made these mistakes, and we have successfully helped them to overcome these challenges. With our expertise and experience, we can guide businesses towards making informed decisions and achieving improved outcomes in their packaging processes.

"PP/BOPP bag is not just a cost; it's an investment in your brand's success. It's the bridge between your product and the customer. Make it strong, memorable and durable."

Here are some numbers to illustrate the importance of avoiding costly mistakes in packaging material selection:

1. **Cost of Product Returns:** On average, businesses experience a return rate of 8% due to packaging-related issues. This leads to substantial financial losses, including expense for product replacement, shipping, and customer dissatisfaction.

2. **Customer Complaints:** 75% of customer complaints regarding product quality and integrity can be attributed to poor packaging choices. This not only impacts brand reputation but also results in a loss of potential customers.

3. **Impact on Profitability:** Companies that invest in high-quality packaging materials experience a 15% reduction in product damage during transportation and handling. This, in turn, leads to cost savings and increased profitability.

A good selection of right type of bags and supplier not only these costs but also many hidden expenses. I am sure you can now identify gaps in your packaging. By avoiding costly mistakes in selecting packaging materials, businesses can minimize returns, reduce customer complaints, increase profitability, and meet consumer expectations for sustainable packaging.

Chapter 5

The Art of Designing Remarkable Packaging

In this chapter, we will explore the art of designing remarkable packaging for woven sacks and how it can create a lasting impact on consumers.

Leveraging Packaging Design for Lasting Impact

Packaging design has the power to make a lasting impression on consumers and influence their purchasing decisions. Think about the thousands of product packaging you have come across. Why do some of them stay in your memory while thousands of others are easily forgotten?

To leverage packaging design effectively, businesses should consider the following:

1. **Understanding the Target Customer:** Designing packaging that appeals to the target customer requires a deep understanding of their preferences, needs, and behaviors. Conducting market research and gathering consumer insights can help in creating packaging that resonates with the intended audience. There are significant issues visible in many PP/BOPP bags

available in the market that needs to be addressed,leading to cost-effective packaging.

2. **Creating a Memorable Experience:** Packaging should be designed to create a positive and memorable experience for consumers. This can be achieved through thoughtful design elements, such as eye-catching visuals, tactile finishes, and engaging opening mechanisms. For example, easy-open bags, pinch bottom bags, matte-finish BOPP with glossy effects, and other innovative features can contribute to creating an experience that customers will never forget.

3. **Communicating Brand Values:** Packaging design should align with the brand's values and messaging. It should convey the brand's personality, positioning, and promise, enabling consumers to connect with the brand on an emotional level. Despite this knowledge, brands and manufacturers often make costly mistakes in packaging that lead to lost sales,which are often overlooked or not accounted for.

Common Mistakes in Artwork Creation

Artwork creation plays a crucial role in packaging design, and avoiding common mistakes is essential for a successful outcome. Some of the common mistakes include:

1. **Lack of Customer Knowledge:** Failing to understand the target customer can result in ineffective designs. It

is important to conduct thorough research to understand their preferences, demographics, and purchasing habits. The choice of images, font scheme, colour schemes, font size and theme of artwork should align with the intended user of the product. Simply using an eye-catching design may not serve the intended purpose.

2. **Overcomplicated Designs:** Complex designs can confuse and overwhelm consumers. Simplifying the artwork while still conveying the key messages and aesthetics is vital to ensure clarity and visual appeal.

3. **Inconsistent Branding:** Inconsistent use of branding elements, such as logos, colours, and typography, can dilute brand recognition and diminish the impact of the packaging. Maintaining a cohesive brand identity across all packaging materials is crucial.

4. **Taking Free or Common Artwork:** There are two aspects to consider in this matter. Firstly, many bag producers offer free artwork to brand owners. However, creating a good artwork requires at the expertise of an experienced designer and can involve 5-20 hours of work, costing anywhere between 3000-45000. Secondly, there is an industry practice where bag manufactures use generic artwork, resulting in a common design that includes basic images easily available on the web. This approach lacks uniqueness and is not specific to your

brand. It is essential to avoid this mistake by ensuring that the design is unique to your brand and that all images used are properly licensed.

Integrating Branding Elements and Visual appearance

Integrating branding elements and visual aesthetics is a fundamental aspect of remarkable packaging design. Key points to consider in this process include:

1. **Brand Consistency:** Incorporate branding elements, such as logos, taglines, and colour schemes, into the packaging design. Consistency in branding helps to reinforce brand recognition and establish a strong brand presence.

2. **Visual Appeal:** Create visually appealing packaging by utilizing colours, typography, and graphics that resonate with the target audience. Visual aesthetics should align with the brand's identity and evoke the desired emotions and perceptions.

3. **Product Differentiation:** Use packaging design as a means to distinguish the product from competitors. Consider unique structural elements, innovative printing techniques, or distinctive visual motifs that effectively grasp consumer attention and set the product apart.

Case Studies on Packaging Designs and Sales Influence

Case studies provide valuable insights into successful packaging designs and their influence on sales. Here are a few examples:

Case Study 1

Laxmi Bhog Atta, Radha Soami Food Products Pvt Ltd

- **Packaging Design:** India's leading flour/Atta manufacturing company redesigned their packaging after understanding their customers and incorporating vibrant colours, a clean layout, and engaging graphics of Roti that highlighted the brand's natural ingredients.

- **Influence on Sales:** The new packaging design led to a 25% increase in sales within the first quarter, as consumers were attracted to the visually appealing and refreshing packaging. Now this design is an industry benchmark.

Case Study 2

Deep Jyoti Soya Nuggets, Goyal Proteins Ltd

- **Packaging Design:** Deep Jyoti, a well-known brand in the Edible oil industry, recognized the evolving customer need and introduced a purple cow for them by introducing BOPP bags in the soya bean market. They created a distinctive and memorable packaging design, incorporating minimalistic and sophisticated elements such as soft colours, elegant typography, and a strong emphasis on enhancing brand value.

Case Study 3

Double Can Khal, Godrej Agrovet Ltd

- Godrej Agrovet, a leader and known name in feed industry, introduced the Double Cankhal product available in 40 and 49 kg packaging of BOPP bags. Recognizing the market demand, they decided to introduce a 50 kg packaging option.

Furthermore, this packaging showcases visual representations of healthy and productive cattle, demonstrating the brand's commitment to improving livestock health and performance. The artwork may encompass images of livestock with shiny coats, strong bone structures, and ample milk production, highlighting the desired outcomes of using Nutri Rich feed.

These case studies demonstrate the significant impact that well-executed packaging designs with expert knowledge can have a positive impact on consumer perception, brand loyalty, and sales performance.

Collaborating with Printing Professionals

Collaborating with printing professionals is crucial to bring your packaging design vision to life. Their expertise in printing techniques, materials, and finishes can enhance the overall quality and appeal of the packaging. Some key considerations for collaboration include:

1. **Technical Expertise:**

   Printing professionals can guide you in selecting the most suitable printing techniques, such as flexography or gravure, based on your design target market, requirements and budget.

2. **Material Selection:**

   Printing professionals can provide insights on the best materials for your woven sacks, considering factors like durability, printability, and sustainability. Factors to be considered are selection of right fabric, mesh weaving patterns, strength of bag, type of stitching etc.

3. **Quality Assurance:**

   Working closely with printing professionals ensures that the final printed packaging meets the desired standards in terms of colour accuracy, print resolution, and overall quality.

Designing remarkable packaging for woven sacks requires a strategic approach that leverages the power of packaging design to create a lasting impact on consumers. By gaining an understanding of the target customer, avoiding common errors in artwork, integrating branding elements and visual aesthetics, and collaborating with printing professionals, businesses can craft packaging that not only captivates consumers but also elevates brand perception and boosts sales. In the next chapter, we will delve into the importance of sustainable packaging and explore eco-friendly practices that businesses can embrace to meet consumer demands and contribute to a greener future.

"It has been observed that printing quality degrades with unprofessional printers because of the use of substandard inks and chemicals, outdated machinery, and inadequate handling of cylinders, resulting in lower customer attraction and loss of potential sales."

Chapter 6

Understanding
The Price Quality Dilema

A very good friend of mine, Punit, has mentioned that even after negotiating extensively with suppliers for each repeat order, there still seems to be further potential for negotiation.

Is this your situation too? Do you ever encountered such a situation? Here, I will help you how to find the right balance between cost and quality when selecting woven sacks for packaging.

It is important to note that polypropylene prices are highly dynamic. To provide you with a better understanding, please refer to the chart below illustrating the three-year trend of PP Raffia grade.

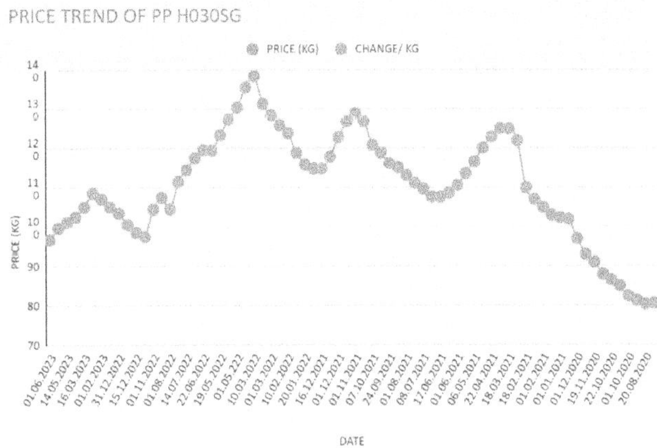

It can be quite challenging to ensure that you are purchasing at the right price while effectively managing costs. We will discuss the factors that influence pricing in the packaging industry and the importance of evaluating a supplier's reliability. Additionally, we will highlight the significance of establishing long-term partnerships and provide practical negotiation strategies to secure the right price without compromising product quality.

Balancing Cost and Quality Considerations

Finding the right balance between cost and quality is crucial. Here's what you need to consider:

- **Product Requirements:** Determine the specific needs of your packaging, such as type of bag, and its strength. For instance, if you want to showcase your product through the bag, you will require a bag made of natural fabric with a suitable window incorporated into the design to display the product effectively.

- **Raw Materials:** Fluctuations in the prices of raw materials used in woven sacks can have an impact on costs. For example, if the cost of polymers or special inks and coatings used in the packaging increases, it may lead to higher prices.

- **Production Techniques:** Different production techniques, such as woven, laminated, BOPP printed, or metallized, come with varying costs. Evaluate which technique best suits your product's needs while taking your budget into consideration.

- **Customization and Printing:** Additional customization features like special finishes or printing techniques can contribute to the overall cost. Determine whether these features are necessary to achieve your branding and marketing goals.

Choosing reliable suppliers is crucial for consistent quality. Consider the following points:

- **Quality Control Measures:** Ensure that suppliers have proper quality control processes in place to meet industry standards. Look for certifications or accreditations that demonstrate their commitment to quality. It is worth noting that many bag manufacturers don't have an in-house lab and testing mechanism in place.

- **Production Capacity:** Evaluate whether the supplier can consistently meet your high-volume demands.

- **Supply Chain Transparency:** Look for suppliers who are transparent about their sourcing of raw materials and follow ethical and sustainable practices. It can be challenging to maintain quality when outsourcing critical processes to multiple parties in the supply chain.

Establishing long-term partnerships with reliable suppliers can bring benefits such as cost savings, consistent quality, and improved collaboration on future packaging innovations.

Negotiation Strategies for Pricing

Here are some effective negotiation strategies to secure the right price:

1. **Comparative Analysis:** Analyze pricing structures from past trends and international PP market. This will help you make informed decisions and potentially obtain better pricing.

2. **Volume Commitments:** Consider negotiating long-term contracts or volume commitments with suppliers. This can lead to competitive pricing and establish a mutually beneficial partnership.

3. **Value-added Services:** Discuss with suppliers the availability of additional services,such as technical support, customized packaging solutions, or reliable and timely delivery, as part of the pricing agreement.

Conclusion

Balancing cost and quality of woven sack packaging is crucial for the success of your business. By considering the specific requirements of your product, understanding pricing factors, evaluating supplier reliability, and using effective negotiation strategies, you can find the right price without compromising product integrity. Thank you for dedicating your time to reading this book and appreciating my efforts. I sincerely hope that this book will assist you in mastering the art of implementing effective marketing and promotion strategies to maximize the impact of your packaging on consumers.

Serving as your guide has been an honour, and your trust humbles me.

Or maybe things are too technical, or you don't have to do research and this in-depth work, but the requirement of a good packaging that stands out makes your product a brand is a must.

Next Step

Thanks for reading so far. I am sure this has added great value to your business.

However it is possible that all this feels too technical or maybe you don't have the time or inclination to do so much research and in-depth work.

But the requirement for good packaging that stands out and makes your product a brand is a must.

In that case you can seek out my help. My team & I will help you get the best out of packaging.

Together, let's create a remarkable brand.

Your Perfect Packaging Partner.

Punit Singhal

☏ punit@jagannathindustries.com

✉ + 91 9680875500

NOTES: